Dog T

12 TRUE Dog Stories of Loyalty, Heroism & Devotion – Volume 1

Compiled by J. Hodges - VIDDA Publishing

www.viddapublishing.com

This edition published by VIDDA Publishing Ltd in 2015. www.viddapublishing.com
Copyright © VIDDA Publishing Ltd 2015

All rights reserved. No part of this publication may be reproduced, stored in a retrieval system or transmitted, in any form or by any means, electronic, mechanical, photocopying, recording or otherwise, without the permission of the copyright holder.

Cover design by John Hodges. Thanks to Barney, our Doggy model.

VIDDA Publishing BOOK SHELF:
www.viddapublishing.com/books.html

Have you thought about self-publishing via Amazon Kindle? If so to make the process easier and more productive, I highly recommend this software to help you on your way.

KBookPromotion: bit.ly/KBookPromotion

Your FREE Gift

Thank you for purchasing this book. To show our appreciation we would like to offer you a copy of our FREE eBook "EASY DOGGY HEALTH: Safe & Healthy Tips & Remedies For Common Dog Problems & Foods To Avoid". To download, visit our website: **www.viddapublishing.com**.

If you're interested in Health, Nutrition, Green and / or Cruelty-Free products please visit our Websites and online **VIDDA Health Stores** (US: bit.ly/VIDDAstore & UK: bit.ly/VIDDAstoreUK).

www.viddapublishing.com

www.sirtfood.com

www.themedicineonyourplate.com

www.greenupyourlife.org

www.ecologizatuvida.com

Table of Contents

Your FREE Gift..3

Introduction 5

Dandy's Day..7

Adopting Shirley..12

Napping with the Neighbor...19

Abby and Misty 23

The Dog Whisperer 26

An Unforgettable Weekend With Schatzie.....................33

Do you want to see the Woodpeckers? 40

Golden Devotion 46

The Bounding Beagle 52

Katie's Dog..55

Her Seeing Eye 61

A Life Saving Nose 66

Before you go..70

Other Books by VIDDA Publishing 71

Connect with VIDDA Publishing 74

Introduction

If you're reading this I can guess that you've either lived or worked with dogs. We don't call them man's best friend for nothing. Since the very dawn of civilisation, man has shared his life with our canine friends.

This book is a collection of 12 true stories that we hope illustrate just why life is always enhanced by having a dog around.

The relationships we have with our dogs are as real and intense as any we have with our family and friends or partners, many would say more important in a lot of ways.

Even though we don't share a common verbal language something magical happens when your soul meets with the warm, trusting nature and intelligence of a dog. All they ask for is kindness, compassion and a regular meal. In return they will be with you through the trials of life, your best friend, always loyal and always has your back when the road gets rough.

A dog makes a house a home and completes the family. A person with the love and understanding of dogs is a person I can trust and relate to, I'm sure you feel the same way.

If you want some funny, sad and heart-warming short reads, cuddle up with your pooch and enjoy these Dog Tales.

Dandy's Day

Two little dogs sat huddling together in a small, cold, cage. Dogs were barking from all corners of the poorly lit room as they sat and trembled. No one knew exactly where they came from, and no one seemed to care. Now that the pair were at the City Pound, their future hung in the balance.

They were found together wandering the rough streets of Stockton, and it was clear that they had nowhere to call home. Both were small mutts, barely a year old. The first resembled a mix between a Chihuahua and a Dachshund with his short legs and pointy ears. The other had a much fluffier coat and looked more like a Terrier that had been mixed with a Pomeranian. Neither would win any cute pet contests, but they each had something very endearing and sweet about them.

The phone rang at a small no-kill animal shelter. A kindly woman from San Francisco introduced herself as Mary Radcliff, and she needed help. Word of the two mutts in Stockton had reached her ears and she was determined to save them. She asked if the no-kill shelter could rescue the dogs from the pound and get them to her, as she lived over an hour away.

Typically, Pet Friends Animal Shelter had their hands so full with dogs and cats that were surrendered by the public, they almost never had room to rescue animals from the

Pound. But Mary insisted that she would make all of the necessary arrangements.

After discussing the logistics, it was decided. The shelter would rescue the Terrier mix that Mary wanted so badly to adopt, and would hand deliver him to her after an overnight stay at a local vet's office. Arrangements were made with the Stockton Pound, who claimed that one of the dogs had already found a home, and everyone breathed a sigh of relief knowing the two dogs would not meet the euthanasia needle.

The two frightened little dogs had no idea what was happening when a man suddenly separated them. They struggled to stay together, clinging to the cage. The Chiweenie looked back at his friend with fear in his eyes as he was carried away and out of sight. The little terrier cried softly as his companion disappeared from view. He felt truly alone now.

The hand-over was made and Will, a member of the Pet Friends staff loaded the confused little dog into a carrier.

"This is your lucky day, buddy," Will said as he set the carrier in the truck. He dropped the little guy off at the vet for the night and headed back to work.

Upon arriving back at the Pet Friends Adoption Center, Will handed over the little dog's paperwork to the office manager. Maggie frowned as she went over the documents.

"Will, are you sure this is the right dog? This picture doesn't look like the one we saw before."

"Of course, it's the right dog. They knew which one I came for."

"Okay…" Maggie said hesitantly as she processed the paperwork.

Will made the trek to San Francisco the next morning. His phone buzzed as he was on his way home.

"Hello?"

"Will, it's Maggie. Stockton just called, they gave you the wrong dog by mistake! They haven't found a home for that other one either, he's still there and that's the one Mary wanted."

"But I already dropped this one off!"

A few panicked calls were made, and apologies were offered. Mary had already bonded with the Chiweenie and couldn't part with him. But what of the terrier mix who was supposed to be saved in the first place?

The staff at Pet Friends couldn't bear to let him slip through the cracks when he had come so close to finding a forever home. The Stockton Pound wasn't answering their phone. Maggie and Will worried that they would be too late to save him.

Bright and early the next morning, Will rushed to the Pound. Relief swept over him as he was assured of the Terrier's safety.

Alone and confused, the Terrier's tail wagged as he was taken from his cage. His eyes smiled sweetly as he was handed over and placed in a carrier. He missed his companion, but he dared to have hope.

As soon as he arrived, Maggie came out to greet him and take his picture for the website.

"Oh he's just adorable!" He smiled and wagged his tail as she gushed over him. "He has so much love in his eyes!" she exclaimed. His thick, curly tail wagged even faster as he lapped up the attention, proving that he was just as sweet as he looked. He relaxed immediately as he could sense his journey had taken a fortuitous turn. He looked around felt lucky to have made it off of the streets, out of that cold cage, and into such a nice, welcoming place.

Dandy-Lion, as he came to be called, settled in quickly and enjoyed his large, private dog run. He also loved getting to play outside every day with a group of other little dogs waiting for homes. But what he loved most of all was the attention. All of the staff treated him with love and affection. He didn't think life could get much better!

One Saturday afternoon, Dandy was happily napping in his cushy bed when he heard a familiar voice call his name. Always happy to say hello, he stretched and walked to the front of his run. Not only was Maggie there to greet him, there were two very kind looking people with her.

He introduced himself with a happy tail and his characteristic smile.

"Isn't he the sweetest?! I would take him home myself if I could, he's just wonderful," Maggie told the couple. "You guys are going to love him!"

"I think we already do!"

Dandy wasn't sure what was being said, but he could tell that his life just got even better.

Adopting Shirley

One afternoon, Dustin Reink's family loaded him up into the car, and drove to a strange place. Peering out of the window as the car came to a stop, Dustin wondered where on Earth they were. His parents were being unusually hush-hush. Hesitantly, he climbed out of the car and followed his parents into a small, cluttered office.

After signing a form, Dustin's mother took his hand and led him outside. Following a short footpath, they entered a large, semi-open building. It was loud, had a sour odor to it, and was constructed primarily of concrete and iron. What is this place?

Dogs. There were dozens and dozens of dogs! A huge smile spread across Dustin's face as he looked up at his parents.

"Now no touching, okay? We don't know these dogs yet. We are just going to look and see what we think," warned his mother.

"Okay!" Dustin nodded enthusiastically. He loved dogs but had never really had one before. His parents had shown him pictures of him as a baby cuddling with a very old looking beagle, but he doesn't have any actual memories of Beau. Beau passed away before Dustin's second birthday. The only real memorable experiences he has gained have been through his grandparent's dogs.

Dustin's tiny frame meandered through the dark aisles that were surrounded by barking dogs of all shapes and sizes. At not quite six years old Dustin stood eye to eye with many of the larger dogs. Tails swatted against chain link, and furry bodies knocked into each other as he and his parents made their way towards the back of the building. The barking and the excitement were all rather overwhelming.

Finally reaching the back kennels, Dustin peered through the gate. Four dogs crowded into one kennel at the end, all vying for attention.

"What do you think, Bud? See any that you like in here?" asked his father.

One dog in particular did catch his eye. A small, red and white pup wiggled and pushed her way through the pack, and right to Dustin. She strained to lick at Dustin's outstretched fingers, and put one paw up on the gate. There was an instant connection.

"No fingers, dear," his mother reminded him.

"Mom, I like this one!"

"Well, let's go outside where it's quieter and we can talk about it." The family retraced their steps to exit the noisy building and went back to the office.

"How'd it go out there, guys?" asked the perky receptionist.

"I think it's a go for the one we saw yesterday, don't you think, Eileen?"

Dustin's mother nodded her agreement.

"Awesome! I'll get the paperwork drawn up for you."

"Wait, you guys were here yesterday?!" Dustin exclaimed.

"Yes, we came while you were with Nana and Papa."

"Why didn't I get to come?"

"Because getting a dog is a very big decision and we wanted to check things out first. We didn't want to get your hopes up if we couldn't find a good fit for our family."

"Oh. Well, did we find a good fit?" Dustin wanted to know.

"See for yourself." Answered his father as a young man walked in the office with the little red dog.

"Is she ours for real?"

"She's ours."

The wiggly young Brittany Spaniel swished and danced around Dustin's legs. Dustin giggled with glee, that is until the pup got so excited that she jumped on him and knocked him down.

"She needs some training, but she'll be a great dog," assured the kennel worker. "She's still just a puppy and doesn't really know better yet. Her name is Shirley, by the way. But you can change it if you want to."

The Reink's assured the workers that Shirley would be in good hands, and in no time at all, everyone loaded up in the car and were heading home with a new family member.

On the way home, Dustin asked, "Why were all those dogs there? Where did they come from?"

His parents looked at each other and thought carefully before answering. His mother started, "Well Honey, some of them lost their families, and some families decided they didn't want them anymore."

Dustin was shocked. He couldn't understand why anyone would give up a dog. His mother tried to explain that dogs require a lot of time and attention, and a lot of people didn't want to give them that. When a worried look crossed his young face, his parents assured him that they would give Shirley all the time and attention she would need.

Shirley's original owners had bought her from a breeder, but were not prepared to deal with the behaviors that are innate among puppies. This beautiful, petite, and smiling pup was given up and put in a shelter because she had chewed up her family's patio furniture. Because of the lack of knowledge, compassion, and patience on her owner's part, she shared the same uncertain fate that hundreds of other dogs faced every day. Dogs will be dogs, and so many people remain unprepared, and ultimately unwilling, to put in the time to train them. Many dogs do not make it out alive. Shirley was one of the lucky ones.

The Reinks knew they were going to have their hands full. Even in the car ride home, Shirley vibrated with energy, and it was clear from her lack of manners that her first owners didn't take the time to teach her much of anything. But Eileen was an active stay at home mom, so everyone was confident that they had things handled.

The first thing Shirley did when she arrived at the Reink's home, was jump up on the couch and destuff a pillow. The second and third things weren't really any better. But she was as sweet as could be, and Dustin loved her already. Their energy levels were a great compliment.

Shirley and Dustin became fast friends, and excelled at getting into trouble together. But with Eileen's watchful eyes and gentle corrections, Shirley's manners gradually improved. It only took a handful of holes, a few pairs of shoes, and three more pillows for her to start to get the hang of it. There were certainly days where the Reinks were frustrated, and there were days that they questioned their ability to cope with the energetic young dog, but they persevered. She actually proved to be as smart as a whip, and as long as she got enough exercise every day, she was remarkably well behaved.

Three months after bringing Shirley home, the exhausted Reink parents collapsed on the couch. It had been a busy Sunday afternoon. Keeping tabs on Dustin and Shirley was certainly a lot of work. It was then that they realized that the house had gone quiet. Too quiet.

"Honey, have you seen Dustin? Or Shirley?"

"Um... Not for the last twenty minutes," Eileen replied.

After looking through the house, concern started to build in the Reinks. Where did their son and their dog get off to now? Finally, they checked Dustin's room. There they were: in a sleepy heap on Dustin's bed. All of the exhaustion the

Reinks were feeling was suddenly gone. The stress of keeping up with a six month old dog and a six year old child was completely worth it. To see the bond that had formed between those two little amigos made everything completely worthwhile. Every shoe, every pillow, every hole... none of that mattered.

Napping with the Neighbor

Michael Stone lived in a quiet neighborhood, with big trees and big backyards. His house was a gorgeous two-story and had high hedges to mute the sounds from his neighbors and give him the illusion of living far from civilization. That is just how he liked it.

Michael also liked to garden. He would go out the sliding patio door and leave it open as he worked in his garden, pulling weeds and trimming bushes. He would cut flowers to bring in the house and decorate his dining room table. Michael did not have pets. He did not like animals.

One day, as Michael was working in the garden, he heard a rustle and looked up. Staring back at him, halfway through his hedges, was an older black dog. Michael tensed. He was not sure what to do if the dog was not friendly. Cautiously, he spoke to the dog.

"Well hello there, my friend," Michael said. "What can I do for you?"

The dog came through the hedge, showing just how large he was, and wagged his tail. Michael slowly stood and backed toward the house. The dog followed him. Michael backed through the sliding glass door, and before he had time to close it, the dog was in the house with him. Michael was worried. The dog was big, and with its tongue hanging from its mouth, he could see the sharp teeth.

Michael watched the dog as it wandered through his home, sniffing and examining corners. The dog wandered into the living room, hopped up on Michael's well-worn sofa and curled into a ball. As Michael watched in amazement, the dog went to sleep.

Michael stood where he was near the door for 10 minutes. The dog continued to sleep. Shrugging, Michael decided the dog seemed harmless enough and went about his afternoon routine. At 4 p.m., Michael walked to the end of the driveway to get his mail. Today, as he opened the front door, he heard a soft thump and the scrabble of nails on his hardwood floor. He startled in surprise, having forgotten the dog asleep on his sofa. The dog calmly walked out the front door with Michael as if he owned the place. He walked down the driveway with him and wandered away down the street. Michael watched in disbelief for a minute, then returned home.

The next day, as Michael sat on his patio enjoying a glass of iced tea, he heard the branches in the hedge rustle once again. He looked up, and he saw the dog staring back at him. Again, Michael had left the patio door open, and again the dog wandered into his house, roamed through the rooms to the living room and jumped onto the sofa, curling up and falling fast asleep. Once again at 4 p.m., as Michael opened the front door to get the mail, the dog awakened, jumped to the floor and walked with Michael down the driveway and away down the street.

After a week of this behaviour, Michael was amused and curious where the dog was coming from and where he went for the evening.

At 4 p.m., Michael stood ready at the front door. As the dog came up, he reached down to pat the pup, the first time he had done so. The dog sat down and leaned against his leg, calmly accepting the affection. Michael slipped a note under the collar of the dog and then patted him one last time.

Michael's note asked the dog's name and where he lived, explaining the pup was napping on his couch during the afternoon and was very punctual to return home at the stroke of 4.

The pair walked down the driveway, and Michael turned left to the mailbox to get the mail. The dog turned right and headed off down the road.

The next day, when the dog appeared, he had a note tucked under his collar on a bright blue piece of construction paper.

On the construction paper was written an explanation of the dog's behavior. It turns out, the dog's name was Batman. He lived at a house about a mile down the road from Michael, and he belonged to a 10-year-old boy named Jax. That boy was at school all day, and in the afternoons, the house became a site of chaos, as Jax's twin two-year-old brothers were at a stage where they no longer napped and were very grumpy as a result. Batman must be seeking an alternative location for his naps because the boys were twin tornadoes that made lots of noise and messes before Jax came home on the school buses – arriving shortly after 4 p.m.

Michael smiled. Then, he laughed as he noticed a hasty scrawl at the bottom of the page,

"Sir, it's a pretty hectic time at our house in the afternoons. Any chance I can come with Batman tomorrow and sneak in a nap of my own?"

The note was signed simply: the lady who feeds Batman / Jax's mom.

Abby and Misty

I am an animal lover to my very core. Growing up I had a medium sized mutt named, Abby. My parents were what you would call, "dog people." Cats were not really their cup of tea. But I loved all animals, and I wanted a cat. So when our next door neighbors on one side moved out and left their cat behind, we took her in. She was a great cat.

A few years later when our neighbors down the street moved out and abandoned a pair of kittens, my brother and I began bringing them home. Only for short periods at first, just to play with them a little. Then we would put them back, thinking our mother didn't notice. Eventually, the kittens stayed more and more, until they were essentially living with us.

Since we already had Cookie, there was no shortage of cat food for the kittens. Cookie wasn't thrilled with the babies, but she coped. Abby didn't mind them at all; as long as she still got enough attention, she was happy.

Despite the fact that my parents were feeding the kittens, I still didn't let myself think we were keeping them. I didn't want to be disappointed. The fact that my mom liked to remind my brother and I that we were only keeping them until we could find them good homes didn't help my confidence, either.

It wasn't until my mom took them to be spayed that it sunk in. I remember telling my brother that they were ours to keep. He asked me how I knew. I told him that mom and dad wouldn't pay all that money to have them fixed if we weren't going to keep them.

Hurray! More pets! I claimed one of the kittens for my own, and my brother claimed the other. He named his kitten, Maisy.

Maisy and Sugar were about three to four months old when they became officially ours, but we had known them since birth and the neighbors left them at only a few weeks old, so the pair had been in our care for some time already. And not just our care; Abby played a role in raising the orphans as well.

Sugar attached herself to me quickly, and while she was shy, she was self-sufficient. For some reason, however, Maisy remained needy. Nurturer that she was, Abby stepped in to help. Maisy bonded with Abby immediately, and Abby took her job as a surrogate seriously.

She cleaned Maisy and fussed over her every day. Anywhere Abby went, Maisy tagged along. When it was couch time, Abby made herself comfortable and Maisy curled up in her soft belly. Abby even allowed Maisy to suckle and knead, even though she wasn't producing anything, as she was spayed herself. She just looked at the confused kitten, accepting her as she would her own.

This attachment continued as Maisy grew. I would walk Abby around the park, and Maisy often joined us. If I asked Abby to "sit" or "shake," Maisy was there learning the tricks as well. They sunbathed together, they ate together, and they played together. Well, Maisy pounced on Abby's tail.

As an adult cat, Maisy honestly behaved more like a dog. She loved to chew on things, and she was always happy to greet people. She did tricks, went for walks, and wagged her tail when she was happy. Abby had quite the effect on her!

Odd couple that they were, it was a privilege watching them interact. Their strange bond that broke the dog-versus-cat barrier has stayed with me and has influenced me into my own adult life. Both have since passed, but the memory of their bond lives on in pictures and in my mind. It's a constant reminder that love knows no bounds, and it can flourish anywhere that it is nurtured.

The Dog Whisperer

Animal control pounded on the cracked door of a decrepit two-story house in Knoxville, Tennessee, taken on by sublime hints by the suspecting neighbors. The strong stench and pungent fumes, wafting out from under the door, and creeping painfully up their noses, was odious. It was ammonia; a testament to the suffocating debris and rotten waste waiting inside.

As was expected, there was no reply from inside. Forced by the echoing silence, they muscled the door open a crack and were met by thick carpets of excrements and revolting filth; a torn up couch spilling foam and slathered with paraphernalia of grime and a TV in the corner, playing news. The room was drenched in murky darkness and the blinds were drawn. As soon as the rays streamed past the officers to flood the insides, a hundred eyes gleamed.

Met by unfamiliar sights, the dogs were frenzied, growling, fighting, snapping and crawling over each other to sweet escapade. The officers labored to yank the door shut but three dogs were successful in squeezing past them and racing off. The officers tackled a few more and shoved them all inside to gauge the uncanny situation before them.

Through the nauseating odors and overwhelming fumes, the officers continued to shout out. It was obvious that the owners were home. Finally, an elderly woman with flying wisps of straggly hair and a limp in her stride came to answer. Embarrassment shone in her eyes as she watched the officers double over in disgust and don breathing apparatus to enter the home. One by one, a noose was pulled around the necks of the dogs and they were dragged out the door. Seeing the sunlight for the first time, the dogs squinted and whined to pull free. Their condition was truly revealed in the radiant light; they were emaciated, displaying grimy flee-ridden hide over lean bones.

Morning passed in to noon as each dog was numbered and carried away; 1…10…56…there were 80 in all! The woman was not only charged with aggravated animal cruelty, but was also sentenced to probation and counseling, and agreed to unannounced home inspections.

The terrified dogs were transported to an animal shelter where a team of commendable doctors treated them for worms, mange, anemia and severe cases of dehydration. The dogs appeared to be cross breeds with short lived family trees. This was especially true of a tiny dog, a striking cross between a vampire bat and Gollum from Lord of the Rings, subdued whimpering in a corner. The brown Spaniel quivered in fear as her matted fur was shaved by specialists, until she was stark bald except for a little tuft of fur on her head, tucked in ears, paws, and tips of her tail.

After three weeks of laborious efforts, most of the dogs, including the spaniel, were treated back to health. Those, too seriously injured, had to be put down. The major question poised on the lips of staff was that who would ever agree to take on a dog that couldn't handle the leash, tremored at the slightest noise, jumped at any attempt to pet or cuddle?

When young animal behaviorist, Kristine Collins, walked into the shelter, in an attempt to befriend the dogs, her presence set off an alarm. She walked amongst desperate barks, perilous growls, eventually stopped in her tracks at the sight of the "Gollum" Spaniel sleeping curled up in a vulnerable ball.

The pitiful animal opened its yellowed eyes and looked at Kristine like a wounded child, seeking solace in the warm depths of her eyes. She suddenly realized what she had been thinking and was struck at her intentions; a big no was hovering on the tip of her tongue, slowly rumbling off to an assuring yes!

The next day, Kristine was traveling with the Spaniel, now named Lucy, secured in the back seat, to her new abode in Illinois.

For too long, Lucy's world had seen nothing beyond the squalor of puppies inside the cloistered four walls. The next day Kristine took Lucy along with her pet dog Juno, to a secluded park near her home. The Spaniel tentatively pawed at the green tufts and for most parts, kept her small body plastered to the muscular one of Juno. After scrutinizing the green blades, she slowly lowered her nose to sniff the ground and her whole demeanor transformed. Ecstatic joy seemed to course through her very being and for the first time, a semblance of a dog reflected on her face.

Slowly Kristine helped Lucy overcome her other anxieties and apprehensions. Since Lucy feared cars, vehicles, blender, vacuum, and even little children, Kristine worked diligently to make her feel at home and secured in her world.

Within a short span of a year, Lucy was behaving just like a star dog. Each morning, she awoke with joy, wiggled her tail, and jumped out of her crate with enthusiasm. Whenever she wanted attention, she would bound up to Kristine, place a paw on her chest and another on her face. She learned to play fetch and race up to Kristine every time she opened the door. Lucy was restored!

A year later, Kristine took on a challenging job to oversee a behavioral rehabilitation center, where shelters around the country sent their most distraught rescue dogs. Lola, a pink brindle Chihuahua, was one of the most fearful of the brood. With trembling steps, furrowed brow and wide gaping eyes, she fearfully darted through the vestibule until she reached the end of her leash and jerked to an unceremonious stop. Rescued from hoarders where she was squashed in a pen with 25 other dogs, she was frantically trying to break free of her bonds and proved entirely abhorrent of any bonding with humans.

Unimaginable traumas had left Lola shaken and entirely susceptible to contact. She growled at her caretakers, cowered farthest back from the slats, refused to eat her food when somebody was looking, and shrunk at the slightest touch as if electrocuted. She was slowly crumbling to pieces and the entire team was stalled!

Since rescued dogs generally felt more comfortable around packs, Kristine broke through the glass ceiling. She decided to leave Lucy and Juno in the penned-in area in the office with Lola for the entire day. As soon as Kristine returned, Lucy happily bounded back to her and snaked around her legs. Kristine raising her eyes, expecting to see the usually crouched figure of the Chihuahua at the back of the slats, was pleasantly surprised to see Lola peeking expectantly from behind the wire pen, tail wagging bouncily in response to Lucy's. Then for the first time in a long time, a sound that sounded like a yodel escaped Lola's lips, instead of a mournful whine.

Their cherished bonding did not stop here. For days, Kristine would watch Lucy passively lounging on the couch, as the Chihuahua rolled around her body and nipped at her ears. At other times, Lucy would curl up next to the tiny shivering dog and wrap her tiny stature with her own. Being stronger, Lucy could have dominated her anytime but she always allowed Lola the upper hand, moving slowly to match her pace, patiently waiting for the Chihuahua to come to her, instead of perusing her. Yes, Lucy was extremely patient and humored her every whim, intuited her every need.

One day, as Kristine knelt to scratch Lucy's head, she saw a face peeking out from behind the couch. The Chihuahua was caught between her yearning to come up to Kristine, and her innate hesitation at any human contact. Twice she tried to come forward, only to stiffen her ears and retreat in alarm when Kristine extended a hand.

The next day, as Kristine sat in front of the TV, with Lucy stretched out comfortably on her lap, Lola tentatively approached nearer without any intention of pulling back. Lucy playfully pawed her and Lola emulated her playful moves happily, her ears perking up. As the two dogs joined their heads together, playfully pushing each other, Lola came within mere inches of Kristine's hand. Tentatively Kristine extended her hand to stroke the soft fur on Lola's head, before hesitantly scratching her under the collar. Lola froze in her tracks, her eyes opening in wonder, replaced by a sweet mild disposition. The magical moment was not lost on her!

Lucy's gentle and persistent disposition had done the unthinkable! Had she not been such an intuitive thinker, she would not have become Kristine's official sidekick!

An Unforgettable Weekend With Schatzie

Schatzie was a goofy dog. She barked at the fireplace, tried to eat fireworks, and nearly tumbled down a hill once after spooking over a swing moving in the breeze. She also had a bad habit of shoving her nose into people's crotches. She remained lanky into adulthood and liked to cross her front legs while she stood. So much for a proud, majestic German Shepherd! Silliness aside, she was a typical Shepherd at heart and was completely devoted.

One summer weekend, we learned just how devoted she was. Our family spent most weekends at the lake where my dad and brother practiced waterskiing and wakeboarding. Schatzie, mom, and I went along for moral support.

We began our weekend casually. My brother and I had a blast being towed on the inner tube by our dad, while mom and Schatzie waited for us at the dock. Our screams and squeals pierced the air as we were tossed, bounced, and thrown about. Schatzie just cocked her head back and forth, as dogs will do. Concern was etched on her face as we came back exhausted.

She hopped off the dock and onto the shore, greeting us in the water as we rolled off the tube.

"Hey, girl! Miss us? Do you want to go for a ride? Charles, help me get her up here!" Between my brother and I, we got our seventy-pound Shepherd up on the tube. After posing for an adorable photo that was bound to be the next Christmas card, we convinced our dad to take all three of us for a quick lap around the lake.

Schatzie was unstable as the boat moved off, but once we got her to sit down she found her balance and almost seemed to enjoy herself. Such a trooper! Her goofy smile was ear to ear as we slowly cruised around the lake. Then our joy ride was over and there was the small matter of getting off of the tube...

Releasing Schatzie's collar, my brother and I slid easily off and into the water. We were close enough to shore that we could stand, and had plans to push the tube up to the beach so Schatzie could step off gracefully. Not one for being graceful, Schatzie had other plans.

Instead of waiting for help, the moment we were off she decided she should bail as well. She jumped. The force of her leap caused the tube to shoot out from under her, and she landed with an elegant belly flop and an impressive splash!

Awkwardly, she found her way back to the surface and paddled to shore where she promptly shook off. Shooting us and the offending tube an exacerbated look, she trotted back to the dock to try to regain her pride.

After the spectacle of the inner tube, the riding dog came to a close, the adults all took their turns running passes through the slalom course. When it was our turn again, I was volunteered to try the wakeboard. Not entirely thrilled or excited, I agreed. I had done it a few times before, so I knew I could get up. It was really riding the thing that posed the problem.

As expected, I popped right up. Ignoring the embarrassing cheers from my family in the boat, I concentrated on maintaining my balance. But movement on the shore caught my eye. Daring to look to my left, I saw Schatzie running along the shore, keeping pace with the boat.

Her concern for me made me smile, and for a minute, I was able to enjoy myself. Then it was time to make the turn. As the boat rode over its own wake, the momentum of turning shot me out wide and outside the wake. I tried to use my knees to absorb the bouncing of the waves but it was no use. I face planted.

I surfaced almost immediately, thanks to my life vest, and aside from water up my nose and eyes, only my pride was hurt. Dad immediately began to bring the boat back around, but before he could reach me, I was overtaken by my dog.

Seeing me fall, Schatzie swam out to my rescue. Poor thing was going to end up drowning us both, so I kicked free of the board and together, we swam to shore.

"I'll just walk back to the dock with Schatz!" I called out.

The rest of the afternoon was uneventful. We gathered up our gear and headed to the campsite. The next morning we had to be up and out early for a tournament, and this time, Schatzie wouldn't be able to come. Some friends who Schatzie seemed comfortable with offered to keep an eye on her while we were away so when it was time to leave, we gave her a pat and headed out.

We had a blast at the tournament and my dad and Charles each placed first in their respective divisions. When it was time to go back to camp, everyone was in good spirits, and we arrived with trophies in hand. Our elation was not to last. Upon our arrival, we were greeted with the grim faces of our friends.

It didn't feel real. The words, "Schatzie took off" were heard but not processed. It couldn't be right. Where would she go?

As the gravity of the situation sunk in, my mind reeled. In my heart, I knew she had panicked and left to find us. The grave faces of my family members told me they thought the same. I prayed we weren't too late to call her back.

Frantic, we spread out and began calling, but there was no sign of her. Apparently, she had become restless several hours earlier and had stealthily snuck away. Darkness was beginning to fall, adding more urgency to our calls.

Dad and Charles stayed at the camp to continue calling and searching there. Mom and I got in the truck and headed towards home. I pictured us finding her running along the road, but my vision was not coming true. I strained to see into the darkness as I screamed out her name, but there was nothing but rolling hills and silhouettes of cattle moving under the moonlight.

Tensions ran high amongst my family. We phoned back and forth a few times for status reports, but continually fruitless calls left us feeling increasingly hopeless. I tried to keep my voice positive for her as I called, but I couldn't hide my worry. I was beginning to despair as memories played through my mind. I feared I would never be able to make new memories with my beloved dog.

The ringing of my phone startled me as my voice rang out in the night.

"Dad? ... Really?! Okay... Mom, turn around. They've got her."

My mom slammed on the brakes and threw the truck into reverse. "Thank God! Where did they find her?"

"She came back to camp."

We sped back, anxiety and relief turning my already upset stomach into knots. Hearing she was found was great, but I needed to see her know she was okay.

When we arrived back at camp, mom and I couldn't get out of the truck fast enough. Schatzie strained to reach us as we ran to her. Dad had put her on a leash, as she still seemed anxious when she reappeared; as if she was unable to relax until the whole family was together. Worried, we looked her over. She panted heavier than we had ever seen, and her paws looked worn and tender, but she was safe and in one piece.

In all, she had been missing for four hours, but it felt like an eternity. We could only guess how many miles she covered, and how far away she was when our calls reached her ears. I can only imagine how worried she must have been to take off like that. How her fear of losing us had driven her away. I know she was searching for us. She thought we were lost to her, and she was going to find us by any means.

That night left a huge impact on all of us. Not only were we keenly aware of how deeply Schatzie reciprocated our love, we learned how far she would go to maintain it. Our family vowed to never take that devotion for granted.

Do you want to see the Woodpeckers?

Barney's ears twitched and he turned his gaze up towards the oak tree canopy. "Bam, bam, bam" and again the same sound from a different area of the deciduous woodland. It was unmistakably a male Great Spotted Woodpecker advertising his presence to the competing males in the area.

As a wildlife photographer and naturalist, the sound of these birds and the warmth on my face of the late March sunshine meant only one thing to me. The seasons were on the change and the cold fingers of winter were releasing the grip of stillness in my local woodland.

Barney, my 7-year-old rescue dog was a mixture of Staffordshire Bull Terrier and maybe, but I can't be sure, a Doberman. He was a proud and handsome dog and as with all mongrels, highly intelligent and responsive to humans, especially me.

Barney watched my every move. As soon as he saw me going near my photography kit he would try and catch my eye, hoping that I'd give him the nod to confirm that he was joining me for the next 3-4 hours exploring the local countryside.

I'd watch him out of my peripheral vision and pretend to ignore him. I'd see his ears stood up firm and alert but drooping at the tips. The end of his tail would be twitching, just slightly, as if it was a tightly coiled spring just watching and waiting to thrash about when released.

I'd check my cameras: batteries charged, spare memory cards, cleaning accessories and waterproof covers. I then firmly lace my boots, still ignoring him and trying to conceal my amused smile because just a twitch of recognition from me would set off an explosion of excitement that would release Barney's inner puppy and send him bouncing and barking excitedly all over the house.

Finally, I'd make my way to the front door, collect my keys and jacket. Barney by this time would be sat obediently as close as possible, looking his cutest. I could feel the electricity in the air from his anticipation and excitement. Slowly I'd turn to face him and mutter in a silly high-pitched voice:

"Would you like to.....?"

His head would twitch down and to the right, eyes bright, almost a doggy smile appearing on his face.

"... uhmm see the .....woodpeckers?"

His head would twitch the other way and I could almost feel his raised heartbeat pulsing with rhythm through his wagging tail.

"So you'd like to see the woodpecker……in the woods would you?"

An explosion of energy would finally burst from Barney. He'd jump up and put his paws on my chest and lick my face, then scratch the front door barking with excitement to be released into the outside world.

Within a brisk ten minute walk, we'd enter my local patch. I know every tree and shrub in this four-acre remnant of old English woodland, and so did Barney. As a wildlife photographer, I guess it's kind of unusual to be out with a dog because generally wildlife not only tries to avoid humans but also dogs. But even though I'm biased, Barney was special. He was like a second pair of eyes and ears for me. He'd hear things before I did and stop and look in the direction the sound was coming from. Of course, I was tuned into this and I'd follow his gaze and wait silently for the beasties to show themselves so hopefully, I could get a photo.

My favorite times would be when we'd find a familiar tree where I'd like to sit silent and blend into the nature around me. I always found this an excellent strategy for letting the woodland life slowly show itself. Just be peaceful and calm and nature, hidden around relaxes and goes about the business of being part of the cycle of life.

Barney would quietly sit with me for maybe an hour or more, sometimes sleeping but more often than not just leaning against me with my arm around him watching and waiting. Occasionally he'd nudge my hand for a fuss, or lick my face but he knew that the purpose of being here was to be the observers. Never was he tempted to bark or chase a squirrel or bird. He was just happy to be with me and sat in nature's splendor.

Very occasionally Barney would wander off to do his own exploring in the woodland undergrowth. I'd lose time being enthralled with something, whether a new discovery of an orchid or a familiar bird that my eyes would be following. When the spell was finally broken, often and hour or more had passed, I'd realise Barney was not with me. I never, ever worried. I'd give a couple of sharp whistles and within a brief moment, sometimes longer I'd hear pounding on the ground and crunching caused by him running through the leaves, crashing through the Rhododendron bushes as if they were not there. It was like a scene out of the movie 'Jurassic Park'; I would see the bushes twitch and move on all sides and then the beast appears and is on top of me. Thankfully the only danger I was ever in was being slobbered to death by my happy companion.

Wherever I took Barney it was never necessary to have him on the lead. He wasn't a chasing, fighting dog. If fact he didn't seem to care that much about other dogs we came across, he'd briefly say a doggy hello, tail up, a sniff of the under parts and then he'd go on his way.

He was great with kids, they'd come over and pat, poke and generally manhandle him. He would just stand and take it, giving me a look as if to say "why are you letting them do this to me? What a humiliation!" followed by a deep sigh.

He'd hang on my every word and command and I was constantly amazed at how quickly he'd understand a new word. I never had a problem with him when walking along the roadsides. When reaching a crossing I'd just mumble: "What have you got to do then?" and he would sit and wait until I started crossing, then cross with me. I never taught him this. The first time I said these words he seemed to understand what I was asking of him. All he wanted to do was make me happy and gain my approval, which of course he always received.

Sadly the days I now write about are long gone. We lost Barney in the winter of 2012 after a brief but fatal illness. I've been fortunate to have traveled the World exploring habitats searching for exotic wildlife and I have experienced many wonderful natural events. But when my time eventually comes to an end and a go over the days of my life some of my happiest times without a question were spent with my faithful buddy, Barney, looking for woodpeckers in 'our' local woodland.

Golden Devotion

Dr. Anna Shane slumped in the break room at the back of the bustling veterinary hospital. It was one of those days. She loved being a vet, and had known that this was meant to be her path since childhood, but days like today always made her falter just a little in her faith. Above all, she loved animals and wanted nothing more than to help them and their humans live wonderful lives together. But that is a dream that is easier said than done.

Already she had had one challenging surgery to remove four rocks from a Labrador's stomach, one severe case of spinal myelopathy that had to be referred to an orthopedic specialist for a cart-fitting consultation, two cases where the owners couldn't actually afford to help their pets (one of whom didn't seem to care), and the worst of all, one euthanasia of a family's beloved pet.

That was what Anna dreaded more than anything. She never made a euthanasia decision lightly, and always tried to keep the animal's best interest as the focus of her decision. The power to decide to take a life often frightened Anna, but she knew it was a very necessary part of her job.

Bear had been a client for years and it was a devastating blow when his blood work revealed that he had lymphoma. The always happy, always smiling Golden Retriever brought joy to everyone he met. He was a favorite among the staff and had become a familiar face at the local children's hospital as a therapy dog. Everyone was going to miss the big guy. Especially his devoted owners.

Anna ran the case through her head over and over. There was nothing she could have done. Some newer treatment options had bought Bear a solid six months where he felt well enough to appear normal. But the suppressed cancer soon reared its ugly head again and one day, Bear didn't feel like eating. After trying a few different things, Anna and Bear's family came to the conclusion that it was best to say goodbye. They all knew that the poor dog's cancer was spreading and it was only a matter of time before he would have been too sick to stand. But knowing the end is near doesn't necessarily ease the blow, it's never easy to say goodbye.

Everyone had sat on the floor with Bear. He looked at his owners with trust and love as they gently stroked his head. That was always the worst part for Anna. The undeniable and unshakable faith a dog puts in his owners. That trust to follow into the fire, the unconditional love that knows no bounds. She always wondered if the dogs were like lambs led to slaughter, or if they knew what their fate was.

She liked to think that they knew. At least some of them seemed to. The thought that they knew they were meeting their end somehow made it easier for Anna. She wanted to think that they had accepted their fate and despite the eminence of death, they still chose to trust and follow. They still chose to forgive. No one can love or forgive quite like a dog can.

She knew there was no way to measure how aware a dog is of what is to come, but she also knew that most are intuitive enough to realize when something is wrong. Dogs are remarkably keen animals and are naturally keyed into human's emotions.

For Bear to see his family sobbing and clinging to him; for him to have not felt well for the last two weeks; and for him to sense the sorrow in his usually confident doctor; he must have known things were not right. Did he know what exactly? Likely not; at least not according to the scientific community. At least for now. But he had to have known that something was amiss. And despite that knowledge, he still thumped his tail in a brave attempt to reassure his favorite people.

When it was finally time, Dr. Shane pushed the drugs and Bear fell quickly into a forever sleep. His tail thumped its last. Anna left the bereft couple alone with their dog for a while to say their final goodbyes, while she went to make arrangements for cremation.

Bear's family had only left moments ago. They now faced a quiet and empty home, and a long road of pain and healing. Hopefully, their hearts would be able to love another dog someday soon. Everyone grieves differently and each at their own pace. Anna was fairly certain they would be back in a few months' time with a new puppy to love. They were the kind of people who couldn't live without the love of a dog. The best kind of people, at least according to Dr. Shane. She made a mental note to have the office manager donate money on behalf of the practice to canine cancer research in Bear's name. They would send his family a card as well. That was standard procedure at her hospital.

Dr. Shane sighed heavily. A few techs wandered in and out as she sat. They chatted amongst themselves and didn't bother Anna. They knew how seriously she took her job and learned quickly not to interrupt her quiet reveries unless there was an emergency. Oh please, no emergencies today, she thought to herself.

She got up and checked the rest of the day's schedule. Nothing else too major was on the books; a New-Puppy Wellness Check, a re-check for a gastritis case, and few other minor medical complaints. At least if there were any emergencies, the rest of the schedule shouldn't hurt too bad. And it looked like she was clear for an hour lunch. Martha was so good at planning and scheduling; she never overloaded Dr. Shane when there would be an especially hard or upsetting case. Anna made a mental note to thank her more often as she slumped back down in her chair.

Head in her hands as she tried to will herself to eat something for lunch, her mind wandered from present to the past. Bear reminded her very much of her own Golden Retriever she had as a child. The very dog who inspired her to want to become a vet in the first place.

"Oh Penny." she sighed aloud to herself. Relaxing and sinking into her chair, she let her thoughts take her back to the dog who started it all.

Penny had been there for Anna through thick and thin. When her parents divorced, it was Penny's steadfast love that got Anna through the rough nights. When she had to move and change schools at only ten years old, it was Penny's devoted friendship that soothed the loneliness she felt from leaving her friends behind. And when her first boyfriend broke her heart, Penny was there to dry her tears. The two were inseparable.

When it was Penny's turn to need soothing, Anna tried to be brave. At fifteen years old, Penny could no longer get up without help, and had become prone to falling. She struggled to rise to greet her owners, pain searing through her weak back and hips. Through it all, she still smiled and wagged her tail. But it was clear she was becoming increasingly uncomfortable.

When the decision was made to say goodbye, Anna insisted on being there for her beloved Penny. She knew it was the right thing to do. When she saw how peacefully Penny passed at the caring and gentle hands of the family vet, Anna knew that she was destined to become a vet herself. Anna swore to dedicate her life to giving as much of herself to helping dogs as she could.

Tears filled Dr. Shane's eyes as she remembered having to say goodbye to her best friend. She knew all too well the pain and feeling of loss Bear's family were going through. Wiping at her face, she pulled herself together. It was time to see her next patient. It was time to live up to the promise she made to herself, and to Penny.

The Bounding Beagle

Bentley was a Beagle, with short legs and long, floppy ears. As a puppy, he came to live with George and Viola Smith. He chewed up slippers and the bathmat more times than they cared to admit, but as he got older he started to improve in terms of his behavior. They gave him more freedom.

George Smith worked as the superintendent of the local school district, so he would leave every morning looking sharp in his suit and tie, and he would come home late every evening.

Bentley knew roughly what time George would be coming up the road, so he would head out his doggie door around that time, race down the driveway as fast as his tiny legs could carry him and sit at the end of the driveway.

George and Viola lived off the main road, so the cars traveling by where heading only to their own homes further up the hollow. Every time Bentley would hear an engine, he would stand up excitedly with his tail wagging and watch. If the car was not George's he would wag his tail quickly as they went by, cock his head as if to say "Good Afternoon" and then sit back down to keep up his vigil.

The neighbors began to get used to his routine, and they would wave or call out the window to Bentley as they drove by.

The school bus would go by, and Bentley would do his routine. The school children loved it, and they knew that Bentley belonged to "Mr. George," so that made it all the more special when he said his "afternoon Hello" to them as they traveled by on their way home.

Then, George's car would turn in at the end of the road. As the engine got louder, Bentley would stand up, and his whole body would begin to shake. He wagged his tail so hard that sometimes it seemed like he would knock himself over with the energy of his tail. George would turn in the driveway and begin his slow way up to the house, and Bentley would spin around in a circle four times, beyond excited that his master was home. Then, he would trot along behind him, getting up to the house as George got out of the car and looked around for Bentley. He would reach down to pat his head, and Bentley would pant with excitement and joy.

Then, the two would head to the house for a quiet evening with Viola. Bentley would lay in his bed in the living room as the pair watched their evening television, and then they all would retire to bed.

Bentley continued this routine long after George decided he was too old to be working anymore and retired from his position as superintendent. Bentley would still roam to the end of the driveway and sit patiently, as though waiting for his master. As a car would turn up the road, he would stand at attention, tail wagging, and cock his head as the car went past the house, saying his "Good Afternoon" in the same manner as he always had.

Bentley said hello to the residents of the hollow, including the school children, until the day he died at the ripe old age of 15. He slowly walked his way back to the house after his afternoon hellos and curled up in his basket, fading away to sleep with a doggie smile on his face. He never woke up.

Katie's Dog

Katie Daniels was born into the world where dogs were part of the family. None of this "animals are for outside" business. Even her pet bunnies got to come inside to play. When Katie was born, her father's dog, Sam was happy to accept her into his pack. He did a pretty good job of raising Katie, instilling in her an undying love and affection for all animals. But it wasn't Sam who opened Katie's eyes to what it really meant to have a dog of your own.

While Sam was a great family dog, he was devoted to Katie's father. But when Katie was five years old, she learned for herself how powerful the bond between dog and human could be.

It was a typical autumn afternoon. The breeze was crisp, but the sun remained warm. Katie was in her front yard playing with her stuffed animals. Sam sat obediently in the driveway as her father pottered around the garage.

"David?" Katie's mother called from inside.

"Coming!" answered her father. Without thinking, he slipped quickly inside the house, Sam right on his heels. Before Katie knew it, she was alone with her toys.

At five years old, Katie knew better than to wander off, but it was difficult to convince her vivid imagination to stay put. Pretending her stuffed dolphin was swimming through the air, she skipped across the street to the park.

As her dolphin learned how to go down slides and ride swings, something caught Katie's eye. A small, scruffy terrier was watching her from behind some trees. Reaching into her pocket, Katie pulled out some stale crackers and outstretched her hand. Hesitantly, the Terrier approached and gingerly took the crackers. Keeping her hand out, the Terrier licked her fingers.

Katie giggled and rubbed the little dog behind his ears.

"Do you want to play?" The dog yipped in response and followed Katie to the slide. The two new friends enjoyed all that the playground had to offer together, running and playing on the equipment. Their joy was short-lived, however, as Katie's parents realized their daughter was no longer in the yard.

"Katie!" came the frantic call of her father.

"Coming Daddy!" Katie answered. "I have to go. Do you want to come with me?" The Terrier cocked his head in response. "Come on, you can come to my house!"

"Katie!!" Her mother shrieked.

"I'm coming!... I really have to go. I hope I can see you again." He watched as she trotted towards home.

The next morning, as David opened the front door to get the paper, he was surprised to find a scruffy Terrier asleep on the doormat.

"Whoa, there! Who are you?!"

"Who's who, daddy?" Katie asked as she peeked around her father's leg. "Hey! It's my dog!"

"What do you mean your dog, Katie?"

"I met him at the park yesterday, he's my friend. We can keep him, can't we?"

"Well, I don't know, we should see is he has a family looking for him before we decide anything, okay?"

"He's my dog, though. I just know. And I'm calling him Ruffles."

Over the next three days, Katie's parents tried their hardest to find where "Ruffles" belonged. But no one seemed to be looking for him. They weren't looking for a second dog, but Sam didn't seem to mind, and Katie was completely enamored with him. He had even taken to sleeping at the foot of her bed.

On the fourth day, Katie was once again playing in the front yard. Ruffles was pretending to be a noble steed for Katie's dolls while her father washed the car.

"Katie, I need to run in the house for just a minute. Do not leave this yard. Do you understand me?"

"Yes, Daddy."

"Good. Ruffles, you keep an eye on her, okay?"

Ruffles just cocked his head as David disappeared inside the house. As usual, Sam trailed closely behind.

Katie and Ruffles went back to their game when a shadow was suddenly cast over the lawn.

"Hey there, little girl. I've got some chocolate in my car. It's just parked down the street. Do you want to come and get some?"

Startled by the strange man looming in front of her, Katie remained silent. Ruffles growled in the back of his throat.

"Ah come on, I'm a friend of your mother. You can trust me." He held out his hand. "Come on, don't be shy, we have to hurry, the chocolate will melt in the car," he said as he lunged, grabbing Katie by the hand.

Like lightening, Ruffles latched onto the man's arm. He bit down with all of his might. Katie's screams were met by the cries of the abductor. He released Katie's hand and took to shaking his arm, desperately trying to shake off the dog.

Hearing the commotion, Katie's parents came rushing out of the house. Sam rushed to Ruffle's aid and jumped on the attacker, knocking him to the ground. In seconds Katie's father was joining in the mix, helping the dogs hold the attacker still. Realizing he was outmatched, the man relented. But Ruffles did not. He refused to let go until the police arrive and escorted the man to the back of the patrol car.

As soon as the assailant was gone, Ruffles ran to his friend. Frightened and distraught, a tearful Katie embraced her dog.

"He saved me. Ruffles saved me. I told you he was my dog," Katie said through her sniffles.

"Yes, you did. You were right," her mother said as she choked back her own tears of relief. "Ruffles, we owe you everything. The least we can do is let you stay with us. Right, David?"

"Ruffles, we would be honored if you would be a part of our family. What do you think of that?" David asked the scrappy little Terrier.

Ruffles yipped and cocked his head.

"It's settled then. Katie, it looks like you've got your very own dog." Katie just hugged Ruffles tighter, burying her face in his wiry coat.

"I love you, Ruffles," she whispered into his fur.

Her Seeing Eye

In the daily drudgery of our lives, amongst the breakneck pace of life, the harsh floods of reality and the relentless pursuits of happiness, it's heartwarming to stop still for a moment and witness something which restores your faith in goodness, selfless love, a rarity, boundless gaiety and an unflinching companionship which blurs the boundaries between two beings. Thankfully, I get to appreciate it every day; just across the street in Clayton County!

Facing our house, the single storied red brick apartment houses two of my favorite people in the world; Nana and Argo, her Golden Retriever. No, this isn't a lapse of grammatical error! Argo strikes us as more of a human than a feral being and his intelligent all-knowing eyes always seem to assert our presumptions.

As for Nana, she has always been this old perhaps, and the heavily wizened pale skin peppered with brown spots, cataract-ridden eyes, the stringy wisps of white hair interspersed with gray over a sore pink scalp, a soft toothless mouth, and her unthinkably stooped stature wonky with arthritic joints, make it impossible to ever imagine that the exquisite young lady with flowing tendrils of silky blond hair and thick-lashed green eyes, adorning the huge portrait in the living room, is her! Though despite her frail face, feeble limbs and gentle disposition, Nana is resilient like a tree, which after every flood, only spreads his roots deeper!

Ever since I was a little girl, I have seen Nana live alone. Stricken with a cardiac seizure, her husband had passed away at the modest age of 71; most would call it an agreeable time to die, as if there was an age requirement for that, though Nana says he lived his full and lived to eat, which was probably what killed him. With no children and no immediate relatives to take her in, Nana had found solace with Argo, her husband's faithful Golden Retriever.

Argo was her constant shadow. We never saw one without the other. The image of the old lady lounging amicably on her outdoor rocking chair, basking in the last fading rays of sunlight, her Pashmina black and gray shawl snuggled around her drooping shoulders, trying to see with her ears the shrill squeals of children playing on the street and the gentle honks of passing cars to drive the children away, Argo standing like a sentinel at her foot, his head in Nana's lap oft-times nuzzling his nose over her hand, has been imprinted on my mind. Occasionally our ball would wander near and driven by an innate instinct, Argo would toss it back, his tail wagging excitedly. Or when Nana called out to one of us to hand over an occasional sweet in her palm, Argo seemed to love the company and the obligatory pat.

In years, Argo had been accustomed to Nana's partial blindness and learned to humor his endearing mistress. She, in turn, doted on him with all the love she could muster in her failing heart. He anticipated her every move and was always there at her slightest movement as if to catch her lest she stumbled. The way he opened the door for an old lady and stood up to make room for her, Argo would have made the most decorous gentleman with a grave sense of propriety! Nana would often comment on how he has taken after his master and sent us kids in a fit of giggles.

The mere creak of her chair or the muffled tap of her walking stick was his cue! He would lope with his good leg to his mistress's side and eye her apprehensively like a mother watching over her tottering toddler. He always sauntered along ahead of her, slowing his stride to match her pace, navigating her paths, removing obstacles from her way. At her beck and call, he would fetch the TV remote for her and they would watch her favorite soaps together. Nana couldn't see them but he had their characters memorized by heart and would be seen discussing their merits to an uncomplaining Argo. He was always hastening to straighten her shoes before she got out of bed, retrieve her walking stick from the corner where it reposed, and in the rare cases when she didn't take her shawl to bed, Argo made sure it was there the morning after. We often wondered if nana ever felt the hampering of blindness!

Argo was getting old; it was obvious from his ever thinning mound of fur and his less than lissome manners. Yet, as Nana jokingly put it, his dying master must have whispered a few last commandments in his faithful Labrador to keep an eye over Nana, because as languid as he was slowly becoming, the lightness with which he bounded to Nana's side defied his age. He was her knight in shedding fur!

Twice Argo had sustained injuries, trying to stand in the way of Nana and harm. Once, I remember a sun-drenched afternoon when a bunch of boisterous kids were racing bicycles in the road. Nana, oblivious to their antics, was ambling on the pavement, as was her way of garnering an evening stroll. One of the bicycles skid uncontrollably to the side and would have jammed straight into Nana, had Argo not bounded in between. I remember my little heart clenching over his bandaged leg, his mournful wailing, and the pampered treatment he received from all the fussing ladies in the neighborhood. Everybody adored Argo and he gloried in it! After two days of a much-forced respite, Argo was back by his mistress's heels.

It has been fifteen years since we had moved from the neighborhood, and still every time I see a dog trailing his master, I find myself fighting back the tangles of times and Nana and Argo are always foremost in my memories. I find myself thinking about them, two creatures as different as they were, bound together by the universal language of love! He was her seeing eye, and she made sure she saw the beauties of the world through him. As I said, Nana wouldn't let mere blindness dampen her spirits!

I wonder what had become of them. Were they still alive, somewhere guiding each other down the crooked path of life, each a foundation of strength for the other? Argo was the epitome of altruistic love for me and although the little silly girl that I was then, the pride and contentment exuding from their home, was never lost on me. Peace and beauty exist, in the smallest things if only we know where to look.

A Life-Saving Nose

Kayla is a typical Beagle. She's happy, loving, lives for treats, and she follows her nose. The noisy little dog has gotten herself into trouble on more than one occasion for wandering off because she was on the scent of something, baying excitedly as she went.

Aside from the naughty things inherent to owning a scent hound, Kayla is a wonderful family dog. And no matter how many holes she digs, how often she noisily demands treats, and how untrustworthy off-leash she is, her family wouldn't trade her or that troublesome nose for anything. That nose that gets Kayla into so much trouble is the same amazing tool that saved her owner's life.

The Pruitt family bought Kayla from a reputable breeder when she was only eight weeks old. No one could resist how cute she was with her big, puppy dog eyes, long droopy ears, and stout little legs. She was the epitome of mushy, cuddly, cuteness.

The family had done their research before deciding on a beagle. Bonnie was pregnant with the couple's second child, and Zach, their first, had just turned three years old. They knew they wanted a breed reputed to be good with children that could serve as an alert dog, but they didn't want anything too large or too small. They had a big backyard to offer, and as a stay at home mom, Bonnie would be able to give the puppy the attention and time she needed.

Beagle's are wonderful family dogs as long as they get the exercise they need, and as long as the families who own them understand that they can be noisy, and are often more likely to follow their nose than to follow their owner. They are vocal dogs who may be prone to digging and wandering, but are usually very food motivated and with proper training, the intelligent little dogs can be taught just about anything. They are generally very friendly and loving, but will often alert owners to visitors with their notorious baying. They are tolerant of kids and other animals and have happy buoyant personalities. Just what the Pruitt family was looking for.

Zach picked Kayla out of the litter immediately. Five roly-poly puppies pounced and played with each other, but Kayla left her siblings to come and say hello to the people oohing and awing. Putting her chubby little paws up on the gate of the playpen, she threw her head back and let out a tiny little howl. Zach giggled as he stuck his fingers through the mesh, touching the puppy's soft paws. The puppy wiggled with glee as she was lifted from the pen and placed in Zach's lap. Zach was immediately showered with puppy kisses. It was love at first sight.

Now at two years old, Kayla was a well-adjusted family member. Despite the fact that she dug herself out of the yard on more than one occasion, and had been a bother to the neighbors with her noise once or twice, she was all in all a good girl. Nose to the ground was how she rolled, and Zach was never too far behind her. The pair loved getting into mischief together and always kept Bonnie busy.

Lately, however, Zach seemed to be prone to getting sick. He missed several days of his Kindergarten class, but his ailments never seemed more serious than a mild flu bug. No one was overly concerned, and no one seemed to notice that Kayla stuck closer to him than usual. The pair were two peas in a pod anyway, and everyone just figured Kayla was playing the part of the typically devoted dog.

She began showing signs of anxiety every time Zach was out of her sight and began baying with greater urgency, even when they were together. Her nose was no longer on the ground, it was focused all over Zach. Bonnie and Rick didn't know what to make of their dog's change in behavior, but the incessant noise and need to be glued to Zach was becoming unbearable.

Kayla never did anything without a reason, and the Pruitts knew this. But what was the reason behind her behavior with Zach? It occurred to them one night that Kayla's nose had never been wrong before, and her almost constant sniffing of Zach must mean something. Worry began to set in as the possibility of something being wrong with Zach other than a mild flu became more and more obvious.

Everything checked out as they connected the dots: her behavior started just before he started getting sick. She sniffed him and followed up with a howl, just as she did when she knew she was on the scent of something important. She acted like she was trying to tell them something and had abandoned the need to follow any scent other than Zach's. They made a doctor's appointment the next morning.

No parent wants to hear that their child has cancer, or any other life threatening illness. Zach's diagnosis was a devastating blow to the Pruitt family. But thanks to Kayla's keen nose and persistent nature, they had caught the deadly disease early and were able to begin an aggressive treatment plan at once. Kayla had known from the beginning that something was wrong with her boy. Her keen sense of smell alerted her to the small changes in his body far before any doctor would be able to find anything out of the ordinary. Thanks to that amazing nose of hers, Zach now stands a real fighting chance at remission, and with Kayla by his side, his parents know they will be able to catch any relapses early enough to fight them.

Before you go…

Thank you for purchasing this book!

If you found this book interesting and enjoyed reading it, we would really appreciate a short **review on Amazon**. All of your feedback is valuable to us, as your comments and input will be taken on board to help us make this and future books even better.

We would love hearing what you have to say. Please leave us a helpful REVIEW on Amazon. Thank you.

Other Books by VIDDA Publishing

DOG TALES Series
Stories of Loyalty, Heroism & Devotion

THE MEDICINE ON YOUR PLATE Series
Understanding Disease, Prevention & The Importance of Plant Based Nutrition and Diet

GREEN UP YOUR LIFE Series (Available in Spanish)
Take control of your health and well-being by introducing Natural, Eco-Friendly habits into your daily routine.

BUSINESS, INCOME & SOCIAL MEDIA Series
How to Promote, Market & Create Business with Social Media

RESOLUTION TO BE HAPPY (Available in Spanish)
Make yourself smile every day and banish stress and anxiety forever

INTRODUCING GENETICALLY MODIFIED ORGANISMS - GMO
The History, Research, and The TRUTH You're Not Being Told

WHAT HAPPENED TO OUR BREAD?
The Chorleywood Bread Process

NATURAL WILD WINES
A Guide To Making Delicious Home Made Wine. Tips, Equipment, Recipes & Foraging Wild Fruits, Flowers & Herbs

www.viddapublishing.com/books.html

Connect with VIDDA Publishing

At VIDDA Publishing, we specialize in electronic, audio and printed books in the subjects of Health & Nutrition, Education & Natural History.

Feel free to contact us with any questions or suggestions.

Check out our Catalog or visit our FREE Video Library.

Browse our Websites and online Health Stores for your Healthy, Nutritious, Green and Cruelty-Free products, equipment and gadgets. Also, for our favorite supplier of nutrients, sprouting seeds and health products, visit **bit.ly/BuyWholeFoodsOnline**

Subscribe to our website now and receive a FREE "Bring Life to your Food" Recipe book.

Finally, you can check out our publishing blog "Living like you mean it" for helpful tips, inspiration and updates on new books and free promotions coming soon.

Websites:	www.viddapublishing.com
	www.themedicineonyourplate.com
	www.sirtfood.com
	www.greenupyourlife.org
	www.ecologizatuvida.com
Health Stores:	US: bit.ly/VIDDAstore
	UK: bit.ly/VIDDAstoreUK
Blog:	www.viddapublishing.blogspot.co.uk
Twitter:	twitter.com/VIDDAPublishing
Facebook:	www.facebook.com/viddapublishing

Printed in Great Britain
by Amazon